Real Estate Mind

Author:
Riccole White

Copyright 2017 by Riccole White

Published by Jackson Publishing
3261 Old Washington Rd Suite 2020 Waldorf MD 20603
www.JacksonPublish.com

Printed in the United States of America

All rights reserved. No part of this publication can be reproduced, stored in a retrieval system, or transmitted in any form or by any means—for example, electronic, photocopy, recording—without the prior written permission of the publisher or author. The only exception is brief quotations in printed reviews.

Table of Contents

Chapter 1 How I Got Started..7

Chapter 2 Learn Your Market 15

Chapter 3 Strategy 21

Chapter 4 Build a Team..25

Chapter 5 Intimate Relationship with Your Finances.....31

Chapter 6 Emotionless Game Plan.................................37

Chapter 7 Revolving Circle 49

Chapter 8 Leverage 53

Chapter 9 Giving 59

Chapter 10 Rich vs. Wealth 65

Chapter 11 Confidence...69

Chapter 12 God's Plan 73

DEDICATION

I dedicate this book to my mother and my children who have been my foundation and rock through this journey. My mother raised my sister and I as a single parent at the age of 14. Now that I'm an adult and have a daughter the same age, I couldn't imagine how she felt at that time having to be a mother of two at such a young age. I applaud her for being the woman that she is and she has been the root to my sister as well as myself becoming business owners today.

Without her spirit and her consistent push that taught us how to develop our passion into reality, we wouldn't be where we are today. Life doesn't have to be painted perfect to create a masterpiece.

Foreword

As a financial professional, author and speaker with over 16 years of experience, I have come across various authors that create curriculums, manuals and books that are purposed to assist those in our community reach their next level. I have had the distinct privilege of getting to know Riccole White over the past 6-7 years. I was able to work closely with Riccole and will forever be grateful to him for adjoining with me and other minority business owners to be a part of my movement called The Real Black Friday. Not only did he provide financial resources, but he also worked tirelessly to assist with the Flipping of a local business within a seven-day period. Since then he has become a good friend and brother from another mother. We share similarities in our Christianity, both as family men, being hard workers, and our dedication to our craft. Best of all, we are committed to being servants to those within our community, we regularly discuss ways to give back to those in need. I have witnessed his perseverance, grind and steadfastness within the Real Estate arena. I am confident that based on the material provided within this book and based on his past and current life experiences you will gain many substantive principles.

I have witnessed his above average work ethic, his ability to build relationships and willingness to assist others with accomplishing their goals. He is a true example of no matter what you have experienced or dealt with in your past, it certainly doesn't dictate your future. Sit back and learn more about Riccole and let him educate you on how to create streams of income and build wealth through Real Estate. Use the principles within this book to assist you with creating a legacy within your family that will affect current generations and others to come. It's just the beginning, stay tuned for many more great things that God will be doing through his and your life.

LaRese Purnell, MBA
Managing Partner
CLE Consulting Firm

Inspirational Words
Joyce White (Grandmother)

1 Corinthians 2; 9- 12
"No eye has seen, no ear has heard,
and no mind has imagined
what God has prepared
for those who love him." [a]

[10] But[b] it was to us that God revealed these things by his Spirit. For his Spirit searches out everything and shows us God's deep secrets.

[11] No one can know a person's thoughts except that person's own spirit, and no one can know God's thoughts except God's own Spirit.

[12] And we have received God's Spirit (not the world's spirit), so we can know the wonderful things God has freely given us.

Chapter 1
How I Got Started

I always had a passion for creating things and putting things together. As an adolescent, I used to dream of owning multiple houses. At the age of 23, I had an opportunity to purchase my first piece of Real Estate. I was so excited that I had the vision of how the property was going to be renovated from start to finish.

The vision became so strong that I began to imagine how the house would look when completed. Somehow I became captivated with the thought of the enjoyment from spending the profit from the sale. I started the renovation off with good intentions. I had planned to have this particular renovation completed in 60 days. After seven long months, I was faced with the reality that my plan had no structure.

There was no money and there was no celebration, and also my plans to go to Aruba and Jamaica seemed to fade away before my very eyes. I remember I had these two empty five-gallon paint buckets that for some odd reason became my furniture during these seven months. They also became my place of confession; I used one of the buckets to sit on while the other was catching my tears. I cried and contemplated for days on why my plan did not work. I had this beautiful picture in mind on how gorgeous the house would look like, and I even purchased flip-flops and sunglasses for the Aruba trip.

What went wrong? How did this happen? How could my perfect plan not work? The answer is, I had no logical business plan; I had no rehab structure, and I had no true end goal on how I was going to grow my real estate business. As I reflect, I think the only thing that was driving me was my passion of not giving up. Passion is good, but without a plan it places you in the pit of downfall.

I finally finished the project after nine months. The money I made disappeared after the piled up bills depleted the profits. My plan, driven by passion, had me in the pit for five years, until the day I filed bankruptcy in 2008 after having accumulated more debt than property value. That was the year when the real estate market crashed, and I thought my real estate career was over. Besides my passionate plan, there was an epidemic that affected me and thousands of others due to scams and predatorily lending.

This epidemic created opportunity, because with the market crashing it drove down the value of homes and scared the lenders away. This moment in history allowed people to purchase homes at a fraction of the cost. I was able to purchase two properties for $9,000.00 - one for $4,000 and the other for $5,000 - on the same street in the inner city of Cleveland. The two properties were a street over from my first home where I used to cry the bucket of tears. How ironic. I renovated one of the homes by myself, because I didn't have money to pay anyone. I only had enough money for materials, so in the midst of this process, I started working for other people as a contractor to keep money coming in.

Three months passed, and I had completed one of the two properties I previously purchased. In the meantime, I built momentum as a contractor. I was doing so well as a contractor that it motivated me to enroll into carpentry school while the real estate epidemic continued.

When I completed the home I had purchased from the $9,000 package deal, I tried to sell it, but ran into a few dead ends in the process. I ended up listing the home on a website called Craigslist. I can remember like it was yesterday when my real estate career began to drastically change. It was my second month into carpentry school, and I got a phone call from someone in Florida who saw my ad on Craigslist and wanted to purchase the property.

I entered into a contract to sell one of my homes for $25,000.00, which I purchased for $5,000.00 and invested $4,000.00. Along with doing the work myself. While I was in contract to close on one of the two units, the same company was referred to me by a local real estate agent as a contractor. I didn't truly understand it back then, but as I reflect on my past, I can say that God was setting me up for this moment to share my story and experience with the world.

I believe 30-45 days had passed, and the man that represented the investment company from Florida came to Cleveland to finalize our deal and interview me. Upon our first meeting, I shared with him that I also had another property that was not complete on the same street. After viewing the second unit, we agreed to a deal on both units, so I reduced the price from $25,000.00 to $23,000.00 on property under contract and agreed to sell him the second property for $7,000.00, which included a contract to renovate the unit as a contractor for $14,000.00.

I profited $6000.00 after completion of the renovation of the second unit.

First unit	$5,000.00 purchase price.
Renovation cost	$4,000.00
Purchase price	$23,000.00
Profit	$14,000.00

Second Unit-	$4000.00 purchase price
Sold For-	$7000.00
Profit-	$3000.00
Contract to renovate-	$14000.00
Profit after renovation	$6000.00
Total profit from sale and renovation-	$9000.00

    I invested a total of $13,000, $9,000 to purchase both properties and $4,000 invested in renovating the first property. After four months, I profited a grand total of $23,000 on both deals.

    This was the beginning of the next level of my real estate career, and the first job that I completed as a contractor for the Florida investment company. This opportunity landed me a long-term job with them as a project manager/contractor. Three and a half years had passed, and as a project manager and contractor I had renovated over 100 homes for this Florida-based company. Since the company didn't recognize my value and only wanted me to contribute to their vision, I left the job and decided to start my own venture. I wanted to renovate my own properties and sell them to similar companies, but God wasn't finished molding me yet.

After the three-and-a-half-year stint with the Florida investment company had passed, there were numerous companies known for purchasing and renovating properties in Ohio. The state had become one of the number one states to purchase real estate at low prices and receive high returns. The Ohio real estate epidemic attracted investors' attention from around the world.

As I continued my journey, I quickly started renovating homes for another investment company out of New York; it was two stockbrokers that saw green in my city. Isn't it crazy how others can see the value of our surroundings before we do!

This may seem untrue, but I met the New York investor across the street from my home in Garfield, Ohio in 2012, and had a conversation with him about purchasing real estate and work as a contractor. Without knowing what was going to happen, I ended up showing the New York investor one of the properties I was renovating at the time, , and he was so intrigued by the quality of my work that within one week he gave me three homes to renovate. Two and a half years later, I have had renovated over 70 homes for this company.

However, in 2014, my infinite intelligence continued to tell me that it was my time to focus on building my own company instead of working for out-of-state companies who came to our city and in a matter of months and became millionaires. I made great money and built great relationships with these companies, but I had to learn how to do business with them that would benefit my future the best. For example, when I was renovating properties as a contractor I would profit on average $7-10,000 per house, which is really great, but at the same time these companies were profiting $30-50,000 per house. I had no choice; if I wanted my dreams to become a reality, I had to step out on faith.

My confirmation came when I had a conversation with one of the New York investors, asking him for an increase in pay based on my performance. The investor replied that after I had made them over $1 million in profit, I should be giving them a discount for the amount of work they were giving me. Of course, he didn't give me a raise. I can vividly remember how I felt after that conversation. It was 2014, in July, I had come to a conclusion that no one will value me enough and pay me what I truly deserve besides myself. After 90 days, I closed out all contracts with the New York investment company and began my own journey to activating my real estate mind.

Chapter 2
Learn Your Market

Learning your market is the first step to getting started in your real estate business. Step one: you must learn what market your state is in. Is it a buyer's market or a seller's market? A seller's market exists when the demand for homes exceeds the supply, giving the advantage to the seller who can drive up the price. A buyer's market exists when the supply exceeds the demand, giving the purchaser an advantage over the seller in price negotiations.

If the supply is greater than the demand, a house would be priced lower, making deals look more attractive to buyers. A market absorption rate is the best way to figure out whether a certain area is behaving as a buyer's market. Absorption rate is calculated by looking at how many homes were sold within a certain month and dividing the number by the total number of homes for sale at the end of the month. For example, absorption rate of 20% or below is usually deemed a buyer's market, since homes are selling relatively slowly and the number of months of supply is high.

Now that you understand the definitions, you can get a little deeper and find out how many foreclosures are expected within the next year or year and a half. Then, you can contact a local lender or bank and ask what type of lending opportunities they have and what qualifications are available. You need to do exquisite reading and research to see if banks are lending to homeowners or if they are making the qualifications hard for people to get loans. It may sound silly, but it is one of my easiest strategies to learn who controls the market. If their lending programs have low interest rates, 100% financing, low credit score approval, and so on, that means the demand is either higher or is on its way to become higher than the inventory of homes. When you see a pattern of banks lending freely, that is a strategy to drive up the market, which brings us into a seller's market.

When sellers are outnumbered by buyers by a big margin and the quantity of properties available for sale becomes far less than demand, such market conditions lead to a shortage of properties for sale. As a result, sellers are able to increase the price in order to obtain better sale conditions, making the market favorable for sellers.

While learning your market, you have to activate your real estate mind by continuously thinking and asking as many questions as possible. Lists of homes that are going into foreclosure or that are in foreclosure are available to the public, and they can be found on your county website or at your county building department. Another good strategy to finding homes is buying tax liens through short sales or identifying homeowners that are backed up on their taxes, but have no mortgage and they can transfer you the property and you can assume the property taxes.

A short sale is when a home is in foreclosure, and both the homeowner and the bank agree to sell you the property for a lower amount of their loan amount. A tax lien is a legal claim against a property for unpaid amount that is owed. Properties that have a tax lien attached to them cannot be sold or refinanced until the taxes are paid and the lien is removed.

There are two ways to capitalize on tax liens. The first way is to buy a tax lien certificate. A tax lien is placed on a property when the property owner fails to pay taxes, and their tax lien can be purchased through the county or government agency. An investor can purchase the certificate for the amount of the back taxes and either start a foreclosure procedure, or, if the owner chooses to pay the taxes off, collect interest on the amount spent on the back taxes. The second way is to purchase tax liens at a public auction. After a property is lost due to back taxes or foreclosure, it is usually auctioned off at a county auction. These auctions are open to the public.

County auctions have been one of my main resourses for purchasing properties. In the last eight years, I have purchased over 200 homes for myself or other investment companies through auctions. The county auctions have been very resourceful for my business. I even purchased one of my personal residences from the auction for $36,000, invested $40,000 and It was appraised at $190,000.

Overall, for my business and personal life, tax liens have been a very resourceful avenue. Remember that not all existing properties are assets to your county or banks, because they have to be maintained, winterized, secured, and have the grass cut, so this type of maintenance is a liability to any large entity. What is an asset to your company is a liability to theirs. This is important to remember while learning your market.

Once you activate your real estate mind and do your research to the best of your ability, you can determine how you are going to enter into the world of real estate. If you want to become great at anything, you must put in the work that will produce the outcome that you envision. One of my favorite authors and pastors of all time, T.D. Jakes, said in one of his sermons, "Do you have the courage to think? Because if you can think, you can change, you can move, you can grow, you can evolve, you can become. You are one thought away from the greatest experience you have ever had in your life."

One of the greatest detours I see people take in their real estate career is trying to find the easy way to success. Keep in mind that anything obtained fast is not sustainable, so educate yourself the best way possible to become successful in your real estate career. Activate your real estate mind and do your research to learn your market.

Chapter 3
Strategy

Once you have activated your real estate mind and educated yourself through different sources, you are ready to determine how you're going to enter the world of real estate. There are many ways you can enter the world of real estate: as a real estate agent, a tradesman, carpenter, plumber, HVAC, electrician, general contractor, painter, inspector, property manager, handyman, appraiser, or just a sole investor. I believe that if you don't want to learn a trade and actually do the work, becoming a real estate agent will give you an advantage. Being a real estate agent will educate you on knowing your market, prime locations, price points, and most importantly will connect you with the people in the world of real estate, including buyers, sellers, and contractors.

A great way I learned to activate my real estate mind was when I became a tradesman and a contractor, which educated me on how to apply and manage a project. For example, as a carpenter/contractor, I learned how to manage jobs and how to complete a home from start to finish. I'm not saying this because I started out as a carpenter, but it is true. Being a contractor and carpenter taught me how to manage all tradesmen because it gave me visual knowledge on each step it takes to complete a home. Being a carpenter elevated my creativity to be able to enter a home and instantly see it completed. It also helped me to learn the basics of all other tradesmen, because I had to learn to build on or around their work, which taught me the basics of all trades.

I am not trying to say that one trade is less important than the other because they are all important, since without the application of one or another trade there is no completion, as there is no "I" in a team... The most important thing about me learning carpentry and being a contractor is gave me the ability to buy a home and renovate it myself, so I controlled the whole process. The purchase of the property and the renovation of the property helped me to save money and make more money at a faster pace, because I was getting paid as a carpenter and investor at the same time. So if you have a passion for a craft, that is something you should think about if you feel you have a gift of being a tradesman.

If you don't have any interest in being an agent, a contractor, or a tradesman, and just want to be a sole investor, it is necessary that you educate yourself on how each trade is applied from start to completion.

As a sole investor, you want to lower the percentage of possible losses and raise the percentage of success when it comes to dealing with the world of real estate. To achieve this, you must educate yourself as best as possible. I repeat: educate yourself. I emphasize the importance of education based on my personal experience and interactions with friends and business partners of the contractor blues. The contractor blues is the repercussion of us as business people not educating ourselves enough.

There are a lot of contractors armed with basic skills on how to communicate with people that have no education on work structure or completion of the project. If you are not careful, they can convince you to sign over your life in the form of a check to give you the contractor blues. When a contractor says he can do everything, beware. When a contractor doesn't carry insurance, beware. When a contractor asks you to put the check in their personal name, beware.

There is a difference between a contractor and a handyman; a contractor should have a company name and insurance. If they can't provide these things, you must put them in a category of handymen and move with caution. If something doesn't go right or if something is not installed right, you put yourself in a losing battle, because you have no documentation to make them responsible in the professional world.

To activate your real estate mind, you must educate yourself to the best of your ability in the area you want to enter the world of real estate. Read, read, and read every book you can find. Shadow someone if you can. If you know someone in real estate, go work for them for free in your free time. Remember, what you put in is what you will reap. There is no way to cheat the process.

Hard work only becomes easy when you understand that it is the only way to achieve your goals. And last, look into a mentor , so they can train you using their personal experience in real estate, but still make sure you do your research. Make sure they are credible, because there are numerous ways to scam, and wherever there is opportunity to make money, it motivates people to lie and cheat. So again, activate your real estate mind with patience so your infinite intelligence can help you to create the best strategy for entering into the world of real estate.

Chapter 4
Build a Team

Once you know how you're going to enter the real estate world, it is time to build a team. First, find a real estate agent that understands your goal and a title company that has your best interest in mind and that provides great communication skills and efficient services. Remember, it is easy to sign a check and have the property transferred to your name, but it is hard to get liens and judgements removed, and that's what a title company will protect you from. They will research the history of a property and give you a warranty deed, which is insurance on your investment that will protect you if any old lien or judgment comes up in the future with a particular property.

Find a real estate attorney that can educate you on real estate laws and the best way to conduct business to stay on the right side of law. One of my business partners would always say, "Everything is good, until something goes bad." Conduct business in the best manner, but never blind your mind to the fact that legal problems come with the territory in business, and situations are going to happen. Focus on the process of eliminating problems before they arrive by understanding the law to the best of your ability with the guidance of a real estate attorney, and as your business grows, you will be held accountable, good or bad. Find a great attorney that can protect you in the real estate world.

Real estate is becoming so lucrative that you have professionals that have been in the business for so many years they have learned how to leverage their experience. These people are mentors or real estate coaches. I truly believe that in order to be a great leader, you must be a student of a great leader. I am personally a hard-headed person, at times believing in myself so much that I skip the process, thinking I can do everything on my own. Skipping the process cost me lawsuits and hundreds of thousands of dollars. I truly believe that if I had a great mentor or a real estate coach to guide me, a lot of my real estate mistakes would not have happened.

Based on your end goal with your real estate business, you need to find your target and define who is going to be your end buyer, whether it will be FHA or conventional buyers, who are typically families that intend on living in the home and raising their family, or investors that look to purchase a home and lease it to tenants in order to collect annual financial returns. You need to know your target market.

If your goal is to keep properties for yourself and lease them to tenants for your own personal goal of creating a residual for your future, you will need a property manager. When dealing with tenants, property managers are essential to the process of building your real estate business, because they will handle answering the day-to-day phone calls for repairs and collecting rent. You may think that having a property manager may cut into your profit, but trying to manage properties on your own will cut into your time. Your time is valuable to building your business and living the life that you dream of living, so think of time as money. That's why a property manager will be the key component if you look to build a real estate portfolio collecting a residual from providing housing to tenants.

Home inspectors can be valuable for protecting your assets. They are trained professionals skilled in property evaluation and pointing out the defects, as well as giving advice on how to correct them, or deciding whether the property is worth the investment in general. A home inspector can be your project manager. He will check your contractors' work to make sure everything is being installed correctly and according to the city code. A home inspector can be a great asset that will help you sleep at night, because he can protect your investment from start to finish.

Your next step is to find a contractor, which can be a difficult task, for which, I believe, it takes an investigator/investor to succeed. Number one rule is to not believe anything a contractor says. Instead, ask for qualifications. Ask to come out to there job site. Ask them if they have insurance. Make a copy of their ID, birth certificate, Social Security card, etc. I'm just joking but in a nutshell, do your due diligence to put yourself in the best situation to be successful and to avoid liars and scammers. Bad contractors come in all forms, genders, and races, so don't believe what the contractors say, but rather let their actions speak of who they are as business owners.

I have witnessed countless situations where work wasn't completed according to the city code or when the contractors ran off with the money. The golden rule that I learned from experience is to inspect what you expect - that is the foundation to the success of your real estate business.

A good contractor will bring you much success, because they can be the infrastructure that you need for completing a job. A good contractor will have relationships with skilled tradesmen that are good in all areas. A contractor should be skilled in or know a skilled roofer, masonry company, painter, electrician, plumber, carpenter, HVAC installer, window and carpet installer, and so on. Through years of experience, they have built relationships over time with good people, who know how to start and complete a job. Good contractors will bring prosperity to your real estate career.

Based on time management and the position you want to play in your business, you can also build your own team by interviewing tradesmen in the professional areas of construction. However, the only way to see if they are honest to what they say is by trial and error. One thing I can say for sure: in any business, if you are afraid of making mistakes, your business will never grow. Believe in yourself and be clear about your direction. Allow your professionalism to lead you, and don't be afraid to lose, because losing is an essential key to having a successful business.

In business, you have to take chances. If a contractor doesn't work out, replace them. If the carpenter doesn't work out, replace them. Even if you lose finances, you gain knowledge of what not to do, and sometimes such lessons are more beneficial to your future than a dollar bill. I repeat, the golden rule I've learned to stand by is inspecting what you expect; that is the foundation to the success of your real estate business.

Once you have activated your real estate mind and started the journey of building your team, your real estate adventures will begin. I forgot to tell you that this team that you built may not produce exciting results in 12 months and you may have to make a few replacements on you journey, but don't let it scare you. Just like in sports, sometimes you have to make a good draft, make the right trades, to build a good team. Trial and error is necessary to your growth.

In the Bible, James 1:2 states, "Consider it all joy, my brethren, when you encounter various trials, knowing that the testing of your faith produces endurance." If you become conscious of every decision and activate your real estate mind, it will lower the risk of making mistakes. Some bad situations we have put our business in only took place because we failed to activate our real estate mind to limit the risk. .

Trial and error is a part of growing your business, so don't move in fear. Mistakes will teach you how to calculate risk. Remember, when building a team, your goal is to become a professional problem solver.

Chapter 5
Intimate Relationship with Your Finances

Relationships are not just between people; you must have a relationship with your finances. It is essential in any business, if you want to achieve success, to look at finances as an intimate relationship. Have you ever truly understood how your sister, auntie, cousin, nephew or YOU have received an income tax check in February, and your account went on this 90-day slim fast diet, and the money was gone by April. It's because you are the person who doesn't have a great relationship with your finances.

Think about your relationship with your spouse or your best friend. You are gentle, kind, protective, respectful and loving, always thinking of the best for them by sacrificing your time and energy to make sure they grow. We do all of that with the hopes of receiving the same back from that person we are building a relationship with. We all know the saying: "Do to others as you want done to you." Think of your money in the same way as your spouse or a best friend. If you don't respect and act kind, the money will feel rejected and push away from your goals. If you are not gentle with your money, you can make quick decisions and make your bank account feel unprotected.

All of these are elements of the foundation, which is love. I define the word love as wanting the best for another person, making sacrifices, and protecting them from all danger. When you are not respectful and kind to your money, you will push lenders, financial institutions and potential investment partners away. It happens because you don't know how to pay your bills on time, which is equal to showing respect for the relationship with lenders, banks, or investment partners.

If you are not gentle and protective with your finances, you will make bad investments, because you are not strategically thinking before you spend your money. If you are quick to purchase a property or business without doing the necessary research, it will leave your bank account unprotected, because you put your bank account in a position where you do not receive a return. If you are not loving and not intentional about building a intimate relationship with your finances by protecting your money and making the necessary sacrifices, your money will leave you and force you to sign those chapter 7 or 13 bankruptcy documents.

When you activate your real estate mind and fall in love with your finances, it will keep you grounded, helping you develop patience and sacrificing mentality. Being intentional about having an intimate relationship with your money will help you build patience, giving you the ability to take the time to research and weigh all the pros and cons before you make an investment or a business decision.

For me, sacrificing became my number one agenda in the journey of building an intimate relationship with my finances. When I was young, and not just by age, but also in mind, I spent money frivolously without any budget plan, strategy, or intent of strategically building for my future. I was in love with cars and clothes, and I was going to every restaurant that had an interesting name. These three habits kept my bank account's engine light on, which kept me in the cycle of always having to fix my bank account to get back on my journey.

One day, a great friend of mine in business recommended me to read this book titled *Total Makeover* by Dave Ramsey. I can remember there was this one quote in his book when he said, "If you live like no one else, you can live like no one else." When I read that quote, it changed my life. It changed how I viewed money. It changed how I valued things. It helped me to see my finances in a mirror, how I put necessities over desires. I began to create a system for saving and spending. I started saving money for each area in my life. I began to save money for entertainment, personal desires, personal savings, retirement, investment goals and vacations.

My entertainment savings were for dinner and movie dates, or any fun event with the spouse and children. I used my personal desire account for the things I wanted for myself, such as clothes, watches and shoes. My savings I used for rainy days, when life situations happened with my home or car. I used my retirement account to build residual income because as a entrepreneur u have to build your own 401k. I used my investment goal account to save to purchase my home and car, because my goal was to be debt free. My vacation account was for me to travel the world and enjoy life. This was challenging, but as I created a pattern over time, I began to see great results

You have to be disciplined when you are building these accounts in the beginning stage. What is in each account will determine what you can do. For example, if you only have $100 saved in your entertainment account, you can go to a restaurant with a budget of $25 per person or a movie and popcorn. I think you catch my drift: don't spend what you can't afford.

One of my major sacrifices is that I went without a nice car for five years, and I only invested my money in work trucks. So I drove a work van to church, out to eat, for business meetings, and dropping off my kids to school. My kids hated driving in my work vans for those years, because other children would look at them saying, "Why is your daddy driving that raggedy van?" So some of my actions resulted in my children getting teased because of how the society views success. My goal was bigger than personal appearances and what others thought about me, and that's what I wanted to instill in my children as well.

I would tell them every time they came home and said they hated riding in my van, "Learn how to fall in love with your goal, and you won't care what others think." This strategy nurtured me to have an intimate relationship with my finances, and in four years I was able to save enough money to buy my own home and furnish it debt-free. "If you live like no one else, you can live like no one else," as Dave Ramsey said.

Learn how to focus on the necessities, and not desires for a period of time, by activating your real estate mind, and you will become a great steward of the process, building a great intimate relationship with your finances. Think of a tree planted in the ground. Its root is nurtured by the water of the earth. Throughout all seasons, the tree sustains itself; in the winter it hibernates and stores up nutrients to sustain life; in the spring it starts the process to develop; in the summer it blooms, and in the fall it prepares for the process to preserve. What is your foundation? Having a great relationship with your finances will help you sustain losses, and you can enjoy the fruits of your labor and save up for your next season. Activate your real estate mind and fall in love with the process to develop an intimate relationship with your finances.

Chapter 6
Emotionless Game Plan

In the world of real estate, in order to be successful, you have to remove emotions. An emotional mind will cause you to lose, if the goal is profit. Based on what part of the market you look to corner, you must apply structure. For me, as a carpenter, I love creating, so my mind stays on designs and creating new looks. However, if you are looking to rent homes for yourself to collect a residual income, or to sell homes to investors to collect an annual return with a tenant living in the home, you need different strategies.

You must develop a strategic plan to maximize your profits, which means marble floors and granite countertops should not be the game plan, if you plan to rent homes for your personal portfolio or to sell to an investor. In 2008, when the housing market crashed and the value of homes went down drastically, it created opportunity in the real estate market. Investors from all parts of the world understand: when there is something tragic, there is opportunity. When you are able to purchase a property for $10,000, invest $20,000, and rent a property for $900.00 monthly, giving you a annual return of $10,800.00 before other fees like taxes, maintenance and management fees (see graph for all details), these numbers become very marketable to any entity or individual that looks to maximize their money.

Purchase Analysis

Investment property
123 Main street
Cleveland, Oh 44120
United States

Purchase Info	
Initial Market Value	$52,000
Purchase Price	$43,000
+ Buying Costs	$0
+ Initial Improvements	$0
= Initial Cash Invested	$43,000
Square Feet	1,300
Cost per Square Foot	$33
Monthly Rent per Square Foot	$0.73

Financial Metrics (Year 1)	
Annual Gross Rent Multiplier	3.8
Operating Expense Ratio	43.8%
Cap Rate (Purchase Price)	14.0%
Cash on Cash Return	14.0%

Assumptions	
Appreciation Rate	3.0%
Vacancy Rate	6.0%
Income Inflation Rate	3.0%
Expense Inflation Rate	3.0%
LTV for Refinance	70.0%
Selling Costs	$0

Income	Monthly	Annual
Gross Rent	$950	$11,400
Vacancy Loss	-$57	-$684
Operating Income	$893	$10,716

Expenses (% of Income)	Monthly	Annual
Insurance (5%)	-$42	-$500
Management Fees (9%)	-$82	-$990
Repairs (4%)	-$33	-$400
Taxes (26%)	-$233	-$2,800
Operating Expenses (44%)	-$391	-$4,690

Net Performance	Monthly	Annual
Net Operating Income	$502	$6,026
- Year 1 Improvements	-$0	-$0
= Cash Flow	$502	$6,026

Riccole White

Buy and Hold Projection

Investment property
123 Main street
Cleveland , Oh 44120
United States

Income	Year 1	Year 2	Year 3	Year 5	Year 10	Year 20	Year 30
Gross Rent	$11,400	$11,742	$12,094	$12,831	$14,874	$19,990	$26,865
Vacancy Loss	-$684	-$705	-$726	-$770	-$892	-$1,199	-$1,612
Operating Income	$10,716	$11,037	$11,369	$12,061	$13,982	$18,791	$25,253

Expenses	Year 1	Year 2	Year 3	Year 5	Year 10	Year 20	Year 30
Insurance	-$500	-$515	-$530	-$563	-$652	-$877	-$1,178
Management Fees	-$990	-$1,020	-$1,050	-$1,114	-$1,292	-$1,736	-$2,333
Repairs	-$400	-$412	-$424	-$450	-$522	-$701	-$943
Taxes	-$2,800	-$2,884	-$2,971	-$3,151	-$3,653	-$4,910	-$6,598
Operating Expenses	-$4,690	-$4,831	-$4,976	-$5,279	-$6,119	-$8,224	-$11,052

Income Analysis	Year 1	Year 2	Year 3	Year 5	Year 10	Year 20	Year 30
Net Operating Income	$6,026	$6,207	$6,393	$6,782	$7,863	$10,567	$14,201
- Improvements	-$0	-$0	-$0	-$0	-$0	-$0	-$0
= Cash Flow	$6,026	$6,207	$6,393	$6,782	$7,863	$10,567	$14,201
Cap Rate (Purchase Price)	14.0%	14.4%	14.9%	15.8%	18.3%	24.6%	33.0%
Cap Rate (Market Value)	11.3%	11.3%	11.3%	11.3%	11.3%	11.3%	11.3%
Cash on Cash Return	14.0%	14.4%	14.9%	15.8%	18.3%	24.6%	33.0%
Return on Equity	11.3%	11.3%	11.3%	11.3%	11.3%	11.3%	11.3%

Loan Analysis	Year 1	Year 2	Year 3	Year 5	Year 10	Year 20	Year 30
Market Value	$53,560	$55,167	$56,822	$60,282	$69,884	$93,918	$126,218
- Loan Balance	-$0	-$0	-$0	-$0	-$0	-$0	-$0
= Equity	$53,560	$55,167	$56,822	$60,282	$69,884	$93,918	$126,218
Potential Cash-Out Refi	$37,492	$38,617	$39,775	$42,198	$48,919	$65,742	$88,352

Sale Analysis	Year 1	Year 2	Year 3	Year 5	Year 10	Year 20	Year 30
Equity	$53,560	$55,167	$56,822	$60,282	$69,884	$93,918	$126,218
- Selling Costs	-$0	-$0	-$0	-$0	-$0	-$0	-$0
= Proceeds After Sale	$53,560	$55,167	$56,822	$60,282	$69,884	$93,918	$126,218
+ Cumulative Cash Flow	$6,026	$12,233	$18,626	$31,993	$69,081	$161,921	$286,689
- Initial Cash Invested	-$43,000	-$43,000	-$43,000	-$43,000	-$43,000	-$43,000	-$43,000
= Net Profit	$16,586	$24,400	$32,448	$49,275	$95,965	$212,839	$369,907
Internal Rate of Return	38.6%	26.7%	23.0%	20.1%	18.1%	17.3%	17.1%
Return on Investment	39%	57%	75%	115%	223%	495%	860%

The Real Estate Mind

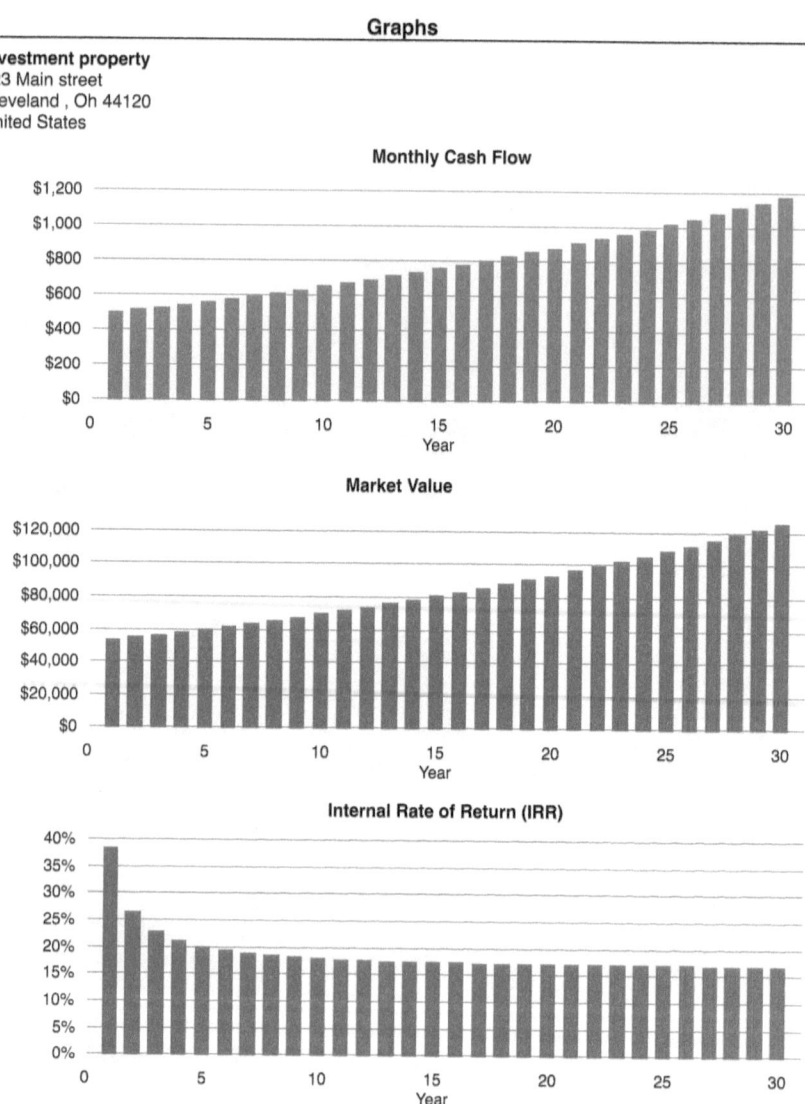

When you look at real estate as purely a business and your homes as the product, you should develop a brand that fits your market strategy. You should replace your emotions with integrity, quality and warranties. This means, if you are selling homes to maximize the price based on the value of the home, then marble tile and granite countertops may apply, but if you are selling homes to rent or your end buyer is an investor, then they don't apply.

It took me a while to understand that I had to be logical going into these rental renovations. I had to learn to create a product that was durable for both the services we were providing and the ultimate end goal of each property. In a rental property, you should create a product that will withstand wear and tear of people moving in and out. For example,, you may have to change the carpet if they have small children or pets, and provide maintenance for certain things that may not be required by city code, but are for personal use, such as garbage disposals and dishwashers.

After numerous emotional renovations, with the help of one of my mentors, I came up with a purchase and rehab structure that systematized my business. First step is, you must purchase right to stay in budget. The exterior of the home can become costly. When I look to purchase a property, the price point is important, and based on the end goal of the property and whether it's going to be sold to an investor or a FHA or conventional approved buyer.

A home I look to sell to an investor doesn't have to be a prime location, but has to have three bedrooms or more to maximize the rent. A home I look to sell to FHA or conventional buyer, I determine by location, market value and layout of the home, meaning bedroom amount and size, number of baths, kitchen size, etc.

When I go out to look at a property, I have developed a militant behavior that I use to determine if I have interest. A property has to have more than one main structure in good condition, such as roof, windows, garage, driveway and sidewalks, and exterior wall structure (vinyl siding, aluminum siding, wood, brick or stucco).

You want three of the five structures to be in good condition, because each area can cost over $5,000.00 easily. For example, if a home needs a new roof, windows and a new driveway, you could be spending over $15,000 before you even start the interior of a home.

If you are looking for longevity in this business, make sure you are buying based on structure and not emotions. Once I have purchased a home that fits the exterior budget, I developed a militant system for the interior of the home. For all properties I sell to investors, I use the same color of paint, faucets, flooring, lighting, hardwood floor instead of carpet, kitchen cabinets, style of countertops, bathroom sinks, kitchen and bathroom flooring, bathroom tubs, and toilets. No matter what my goal is with a property, I replace the main mechanics such as HVAC, plumbing, and electrical, because these are the high cost issues you want to rectify in the beginning.

Once the exterior mechanics are up to code, your everyday maintenance is your interior mechanics, which you want to address in the beginning. When you replace the furnace in a home you're going to rent, you eliminate those late night calls about the furnace not working in those cold winter nights. All new furnaces come with a 5-year to 10-year warranty and options to extend warranty. This secures you with one less headache, and because nothing is perfect, if something goes wrong, the company replaces parts under the warranty. When you update the electrical to code, you eliminate complaints of fuses blowing or your tenants having to use 2-prong adapters because you don't have updated plugs.

Plumbing is changed based on each particular property. If you purchase a home and it has galvanized water lines, I replace those without question, regardless if it is working or not. Reason being that galvanized lines rust inside out, so if you purchase a home that's been sitting for a while, those line tend to rust and contaminate the water. In most homes I buy, I would say over 75%, thieves steal the plumbing. My replacement option is either cpvc or pex, which both are plastic and highly durable. If you have a home that has copper water lines, I keep them as long as the home hasn't been vacant for a while. I live in Ohio, and if a home is vacant during the winter, it causes the pipes to swell and bust or eventually burst once water pressure is applied. In order to save money and headaches in the beginning, I would add to the renovation budget to change out all water lines.

You may find a home that doesn't have any issues, but if you are looking for long-term solution, apply the changes. I would personally say, in over 60% of the homes, I used to keep the plumbing, because it was working fine in the beginning, I eventually had to go back while a tenant was occupying the property to cut open walls to replace a water line.. If you look to have longevity in this business, eliminate any issues you can in the beginning to eliminate the headaches six-seven months down the road. I also look to change all waste drains. Find a professional who you can pay to use a camera and clean the drains to determine if they are working properly. I learned this from trial and error, so to save you from the stress and possibly running from the business, follow the process of elimination upfront.

When you have all the mechanics of the property covered, then you find one specific tile that is neutral and not expensive, but adorable. Use it to cover the major floor for every house. Next, find a paint color for all homes, then find a brand of faucet and make that faucet the same, and so on. Once you find a list of materials you are going to use to create a brand of homes, it will put everything in perspective. I call this an economy rehab, which doesn't have high-end materials, but they are durable. When a tenant moves out of the property, and you have an issue, you know exactly who to call and what to do. Either you have a warranty or you have leftover material in stock, or you know exactly what to buy, because you already have a list.

Putting a system in place will give your business advantage on the road to become successful, because it puts you in a position where there is no "should change it" in order to maintain the units. I like to call it the Ford Motors blueprint of real estate. This plan covers all bases; if you sell to an investor, you're able to sell with warranties and have a list of all materials you will need for management purposes. It's a win-win situation for you as the owner, as well as for the tenant, and for the potential investor.

My second product type of home is what I like to call my signature homes. It is a home that is put on the market and sold through FHA or conventional lending. After the market crashed in 2008, banks weren't lending. I know people that have been renting for the past 9 years are potential buyers. If you want to create age in this market, activate your real estate mind. You must develop a strategy to develop a strong business.

I created what I call a home, and I developed a signature home strategy cost by studying my competition and up-to-date styles of renovations. What are you looking for to create your signature home? First, you want to find out the average sales price in the area you are looking to buy. If a home is listed with a brokerage, it's public record. View the style of renovation, or even better, go to the open house of a home that is in an area that you have identified. Look at the amenities in these homes, such as kitchen styles, bathroom styles, finished basements, extra baths, central air, windows, etc. You can get great ideas from magazines and rehab sitcoms. Activate your real estate mind and become creative in your research to craft your own style and price your signature homes at the same affordable prices as your competition.

To become great, you have to become unique, so learn how to be creative within your budget, so that your homes stand out and sell faster than your competition. Becoming creative will catch the eye of a traditional family, where the woman is looking for style in the kitchen and bath and the man is thinking about the budget and his man cave. If you can create a product to speak to both the man's and woman's needs, your product will catch their eyes and their bank account.

The key to creating your strategic game plan is learning your market, creating a strategic strategy, and most importantly removing the emotional thinking, if it doesn't add to the check or duplicating your brand, it does not transfer into currency. Activate a real estate mind and key in on your strategy, and become militant to your end goal to flourish your real estate business.

Chapter 7
Revolving Circle

Life is a forever-growing process made up of good and bad experiences to direct your path. In my journey of life, I have learned a few main factors that became a light bulb in my mind about two years ago. Up to a certain point in my life, I thought I was doing well, and based on where I came from, I thought the sky was the limit. Because of the success I had in previous years, I had created these projections for my next season of business to come in systematically. As I created them, my mind and creativity excited me, because all I could see was success.

As we all know, projections are only educated guesses based on the current business history. My projections became like an over-budgeted Christmas list; they just didn't happen, and I began to move in this revolving circle of moving fast, but gaining slow. While traveling in the circle of life, lessons were gained in the good times of business and in the bad times of business. I learned that not every gain in life has to have a check attached to it. Note: if you want to be successful in anything in life, you must learn to look at the good and bad times in your personal life and your business the same way. We only look at life from one vision. We only relate business achievements to a financial gain, but what really keeps us climbing in our career and personal lives is lessons. From my experience, most lessons that I paid the closest attention to have been through lost finances in some shape or form.

In the Bible of the book of James 1:2-3 states, "Consider it nothing but joy, my brothers and sisters, whenever you fall into various trials. Be assured that the testing of your faith {through experience} produces endurance {leading to spiritual maturity and inner peace} and let endurance have its perfect results and do a thorough work, so that you may be perfect and completely developed in your faith lacking nothing."

I believe this word is universal to life, no matter what religion you are. This scripture gave me the understanding of how to deal with downtimes in your business and personal life. I learned how to look at losses as a gain which is more valuable than money. Will you establish balance in your life? I understand that money is only an element created from your foundation, and your foundation is developed by your wisdom, and wisdom is only obtained by life experiences, good and bad. Activate your real estate mind and remove the fear of losing. The revolving circle is that place in your life where you fear moving forward with your dreams and goals. Learn to believe in yourself and understand that losing is part of the plan.

Chapter 8
Leverage

When I came out of my revolving circle, my experience gave me two key components that helped me to activate my real estate mind: leverage and giving. Leverage should be the foundation to your wealth-building. The revolving circle is created in your life when you try to become a master in every field of your business, or when with every digit on that check, you only look forward to only increasing your bank account. Trying to become a master in every area weakens the area you produce the best in. This is the main reason why we fail and give up, lose the business, or just try another field of business. In the construction field, I had a hard battle as a carpenter, investor, home inspector, and all the other hats I wore in the beginning of the learning stage of business.

Being skilled in multiple areas helped me, because at times when I couldn't afford to hire someone to complete a task, I had the ability to complete the task at hand. It worked out well until a certain point, and then a certain point came when I wanted to grow from doing one house at a time to two or three at a time. There wasn't enough time in a day to be the carpenter/project, manager/secretary/investor, etc. After I exerted all my energy, and those five cups of coffee no longer kept me going, it became my downer, and I crashed.

I would put myself in situations where I would be almost 90% complete with a home, but personally I was mentally, spiritually, physically, and financially drained, and those are those moments in life when you contemplate about giving up. I can say I've been in that place in business 3-4 times, and the only reason that stopped me from buying a hot dog stand or getting a 9-to-5 was my relationship with God. Moreover, it was my knowledge that building homes wasn't just my business; it was my passion. No matter the direction of my life, it has always been clear to me that real estate was my passion. I just had to continue to pray, so I could find an answer to solving my issues.

Four years ago, a thought came to my mind. It was so simple that I couldn't believe that the answer was so close to me. Have you ever been at a time in life where you were so sure you were making the right turn in life that you ended up turning down the wrong street? Those are the moments when God is trying to tell you to slow down and humble yourself, so you can listen to the inner voice that you always tune out due to all these self-afflicted disturbances in our lives. We, as humans, can create these drowning situations in our lives, and the first person we call is God. What I've learned is that God equipped us with so much power and resources that we can only activate his power after we use all of the critical thinking and power he put in us.

God said that we are heirs in his likeness, which means we are created in his image and we possess the same power he created the Earth with. God created the Earth with his mouth by speaking it out into existence, and since we are heirs in his likeness, we possess the same power of creation with our mouths. I only say this based on my own personal experience; God doesn't come when I call, when it's a situation he equipped me with the power to achieve. He only comes when there is a situation where a miracle needs to be performed or after I've done everything in my power. Based on my past failures and successes in mediocre years, this understanding became very clear to me and that was leverage. I understood the power to a certain degree of business relationships, but at the time, it was clear as day, as I can remember. I was sitting in my car at a place I usually went to think. It was a parking lot of a restaurant that was set on a hill. From the parking lot, you could look over a cliff and you could see the city for miles away. I would come to this place when my mind was heavy. I would sit in silence and ponder over my good and bad choices in life. Leverage is what spoke out to me, and it became clear to me that I had to restructure my business around leverage.

I live in the great city of Cleveland, so I have to mention the greatest athlete on the planet LeBron James. Lebron was drafted by the Cavaliers, and instantly became a superstar; in an 82-game season he was spectacular. He couldn't be stopped. Three seasons into his career, they were comparing him with the greatest player to step into the arena before him, but his first time with the Cavs, he couldn't win a championship. He had a good supporting cast, but not all of them shared the same goal or put in the work to reach their full potential. You can't build a championship team where each player doesn't share the same goal. So LeBron had taken his talents to South Beach, and after two championships, he came back home after Dan Gilbert, the owner understood he had to build a strong like-minded team. Get the message clearly; you have to build a team around the people who understand their role on the team.

You have to be like a scout and go out, see players practice, learn how their minds work, and what their goals in life are. If their objective is only to make money or have tangible things, you may not ever win a championship. You may get to the playoffs, but never taste the true meaning of life. Money is important, but it is not the foundation to building a strong team. Money is a byproduct of you or your brand, and your brand is a mirror image of your character. When you are building, you have to look deeper than what you see. Activate your real estate mind and use your infinite intelligence. Add piece to the process; don't be afraid to lose, because losing is the key to winning, if you continue your journey.

Once you know your direction in your journey, become intentional about building with others. Leveraging yourself in business will give you a platform and opportunities you may not have access to. Six years ago, when I was building my brand and looking to elevate my company, I worked for a nonprofit organization. They gave me jobs as a contractor in their community through a grant program. As I continued to build trust with the head director of the program, I learned that, because they were a non-profit organization, they had relationships with other non-profit entities, and the other entities had access to properties. Because of this relationship, I received the ability to purchase properties by the bulk at low cost.

The result of building that relationship, based on my integrity and good work, gave me access to the organization's resources and gave them access to my resources. This is called leverage. This is a great example that wealth is only developed through building of personal and business relationships. If you are looking to take your personal and business life to the next level, you must be intentional about building great relationships. You must understand that one may be stronger in one area, while you may be stronger in another, but together you can both enjoy the fruit of each other's talents. Activate your real estate mind and be intentional about building great relationships.

Chapter 9
Giving

Oh, the joys of those who are kind to the poor. The law rescues them when they are in trouble. The Lord protects them and keeps them alive. He gives them prosperity in the land, and rescues them from their enemies. The Lord nurses them when they are sick and restores them to health.

-Psalms 41: 1-3

I've always had a passion to give to children living in poverty when I was growing up. I believe the drive came from me growing up fatherless and in a poor environment. As a child, being raised in a non-traditional home, I grew up based on what I saw in my environment. I developed a heart for people, animals, and places. Whatever is that special thing that touches your heart, that gives you that burning desire to help others - never let go of that feeling. You must learn to develop that feeling and transform it into actions. I believe that everything in life is designed to transform your talent into wealth and to giving to those people or places in need.

And God bless them, and God said unto them, be fruitful, and multiply, and replenish the earth, and subdue it: and have dominion over the fish in the sea in the fires in the sky and over every living creature that moves on the ground.

-Genesis 1: 28

I'm not a scholar, but when I read this scripture, it stands out to me as the foundation of life. *Fruitful* represents your gift, talent. *Multiply* represents putting your talent, gift, to work to produce a return to build wealth. *Replenish* represents restoring whatever is lacking and supplying to your world what God has given you the ability to see. *Subdue the earth* represents the reaping of the cycle, giving you dominion and respect wherever you go on earth.

For me, this cycle is clear; using all your resources to leverage your gift to replenish the earth, which is the key to having a wealthy life. Find your passion and learn how to transform your passion into a business, because if you follow these two steps, it will not feel like work anymore. If your career in business lines up with your passion, your mind will be creative naturally, because your passion is what's inside your heart. Passion excites you; it makes you rise up in the morning with excitement. Passion makes you stay up late nights without counting every minute on your mental time clock.

When your passion and business become one and matrimony, whatever you do will become effortless, because your hard work will transform into capital, business relationships, leverage through streams of income, and generational wealth. This is what I call the multiplier effect. Once you identify your passion and truly believe in yourself, that energy and hard work will attract others to believe in you as well. This is what I defined as leverage using all resources and relationships to multiply.

Life has taught me in my real estate journey through experience that there is one system, a universal law that can be applied not just to business, but personal life as well, no matter what direction you take as an entrepreneur. When I went to school for carpentry, I learned the step-by-step system you must follow, and you cannot skip a process within that system. You can't complete step one, skip steps two and three and then jump to step four. That will only create subtraction and put you back to step one. If you skip step three after you multiply, it will cause you to decrease, and not increase.

Once I found my passion and identified how to develop it into a business, it multiplied, because the hard work became easy. I was doing what I loved to do, which is creating and building. For several years, I have been on a straight path and could see exactly where I was going. Then, somehow my straight path turned into a revolving circle, where there is a period of no growth spiritually, mentally, physically or financially. Then, somehow I would end back at step one trying to redirect my passion to another road, but I continued to somehow find myself back in the revolving circle.

As I continued to contemplate on how I ended up in the same position, it came to me that I wasn't following the system consistently. That's when it clicked; I had to have the same energy for every step of the system equally, in order to escape the revolving circle. When my mind truly understood the meaning of *replenish* to its full extent, it became clear that whatever God allows me to gain, whether it's money, knowledge or time, I will share it with those who He let me encounter. When my heart and mind became one with this thought and I applied it to my actions, it resulted in such experience as if I was in heaven on earth. It is the most gratifying feeling, to be able to give your time, energy, and finances to those in need. When I experienced it wholeheartedly with the right intentions, I instantly wanted to continue to have that experience for the rest of my life.

When you become fruitful, your passion is developed into a business, and you begin to *multiply* and *replenish* the earth with what God blessed you, it leads you to completion of the system, which is, *subdue* the earth. When God said subdue the earth, He meant taking control of using all the resources HE gave you access to. It will give you a great name on earth. It will give you respect and honor. I can only speak from my experience, based on how I've seen life through my upbringing. I know, I wanted to change the dynamics of my family by creating a great last name and generational wealth, where my children and their children will not have to worry about the basic necessities of life. When food, clothing, and shelter are at risk, life can cause you to live in fear, creating habits of becoming comfortable with not having.

If you follow these simple steps, you will create a pattern of success. When the basic foundation is not at risk, it will teach children to use their minds to develop their passions instead of praying there's food in the refrigerator.

If you are serious about changing your life and your children's lives, activate your real estate mind and become one with these simple steps to become what God created you to be. I've learned through experience that you will continue to only see your dreams in your mind, and they will not be manifested in your life if you don't follow the system. Don't become the one who has to continue to start over every time just to end up in the revolving circle. Continue on the straight path and live your life as your mind imagines it.

Chapter 10
Rich vs. Wealth

Rich (adj.) - a person that doesn't understand how to build wealth and is destined to go broke for lack of knowledge.

All my life I stored in my mind that I wanted to be rich, without understanding the difference between being rich and wealthy. I was surrounded by strong-hearted people that had no guidance on how to build wealth, because of lack of knowledge on how to change the dynamics of life. All I would think about, as a child, is that I didn't want to starve or walk around being teased because of holes in my clothes and shoes. Up until 10 years ago, I chased the life of being rich, so I would not starve or be judged by my personal appearance. It was already enough that I was overweight as a child, but to be overweight and walk around with dirty clothes on just didn't settle with my soul. My mentality was built on the thought that I didn't want to struggle instead of focusing on grades and academics.

Confused by a combination of a lack of knowledge and survival skills, I was lost. From the age of 13 to the age of 27, this illusion kept me chasing life and only walking around the world tasting samples of what I thought would change my life. When I finally thought I got out of the maze of struggle and had a glimpse of stability, I was sitting in my home we had purchased five years prior to filing bankruptcy, and I realized that I had to change my thinking.

What I was chasing was not based on God's plan, but it was driven by fear of my children being characters of my past. I quickly began to understand that the desire to become rich wasn't the key to having a blessed life. It was an illusion that imprisoned my mind to chase gratification and acceptance from the world. I came to terms with the idea that chasing the dream of becoming rich equals mental imprisonment. I defined the word rich as having a certain amount of money that brings you comfort, but only results in becoming broke after seeking the approval of others and the gratification of feeling of value.

Wealth (adj.) - a balance of life, strategically using your gift and resources to build relationships, and residuals with a continuation of multiplication.

I believe that a wealth state of mind equals true freedom in every area of your life mentally, spiritually, physically, and financially. Wealth is not just having a large sum of money and tangible things that decrease in value. Wealth is working hard in every area of your life, creating a habit of balancing, and not making one area more important than others.

The first thing I had to do to understand the world is removing the thought appearing in my mind with the image of a pot of gold and a 10,000-square-foot house with every car I could imagine. Although that sounds nice, and there are things I want to obtain, I have to put in perspective that money is only the byproduct of operating the system from chapters 9 and 10. Imagine a tree that was planted in the ground and it grows based on being fed by a stream of water. That tree grows strong and produces leaves every season: winter, spring, summer and fall.

2. Who delights in the law of the lord, and who meditates on his law day and night. 3. That person is like a tree planted by streams of water, which yields its fruit in season and whose leaf does not wither- whatever they do will prosper.

-Psalm 1: 2-3

Leaves fall and grow every season. Imagine that leaves represent money and the foundation is the root that is planted in the ground, which represents your business or brand. If your focus is on the leaves that fall to the ground and die, and not the root that was planted by the stream of water, you will never prosper. You can't water a leaf and make it grow, but if you feed a root, and it can grow leaves. We must stop spending our money on things that will not bring us returns. Instead, we should try to learn how the stock market works and invest in residential and commercial real estate.

Leverage your gift with like-minded others that have a gift, so you both can utilize the help of each other to generate wealth. Think long-term. This may sound crazy, but get insurance policies on the elderly in your family; believe it or not, this is how wealth is transferred to the next generation of your family. Activate your real estate mind and become creative in your thinking. Do your research and remove the thoughts of becoming rich. Replace them with the thoughts of becoming wealthy.

Chapter 11
Confidence

I remember being at a family function, surrounded by these educated people who believed that there is only one way to become successful. We were all sharing our dreams and goals for the future, and as everyone began to share how they wanted to be a doctor or engineer, they also spoke on how many years it would take. I could remember being excited to be around people whose life highlights were not just about having a new pair of Jordans or the hottest clothing.

Then it seemed to be my turn, and as I shared my views on how I wanted to be an investor and sale real estate and own my home debt free, I didn't see the same excitement as I had for their dreams. I remember as it was yesterday, as it felt like a cold day in 90° summer weather. I felt like the music stopped and the whole gathering event was focused on my story on how I was going to build a business with having a GED instead a 4.0 GPA. I watched as their mouths dropped with disbelief, as I shared that my goal didn't require eight years of college, but the amount of success was equivalent to the end result of their goals.

This was the day I pledged to myself that no matter what people say, I will believe in myself until I die. We have been taught in our society that the only way to success was to go to grade school, then to college for an unknown amount of years, and only afterwards life would be prosperous. I agree that education is a must, but I also agree that based on whatever your passion in life is, you should find out what education is required to develop that into a business. I believe that once you know what makes you come alive and you find out how to turn it into a business or a career, that's the direction of education you should take. Whether it's getting a certificate in a specific training or going to school for eight years, you should decide depending on your passion.

I call this direct education. Whatever you desire to do in life, that's the education or field you should get training in. If you want to be a doctor, it may take you eight years of college, so that's what you should do. If you want to be a builder, then you should go get the right training to receive your certificate.

One thing I've learned in life is that as long as people are living, you will need a doctor, and as long as people are being born into this world, you will need brick and mortar to build roads to travel and homes to live in. I have respect and honor for both crafts and believe they both are essential to our lives. Both of these crafts can produce the same type of living if it's your passion. You just have to have confidence in yourself. I believe education is mandatory and continuing education is essential to your goals, because every day things evolve and change, but being direct with your education will bring out your passion.

You must develop confidence in yourself that no one can take away from you. Discover the key components inside you, no matter if a person, place, or moment in your life impact you negative or positive. Everything you need to succeed is inside you; it is up to you to develop it. The earth was created by God speaking it into existence, when he said light, there light appeared. Then he spoke man into existence and said, you are my heir, a person who inherits the power or gift of the one who created them.

Just think; if God created the earth by speaking it into existence and he said, you are my heir, that means we have the same power to create our dreams into existence; we just have to believe and speak. Your mouth has the power to give life to your future, if you speak it and demonstrate it with your actions. Have confidence in yourself. Remember, it's not how you start; it's how you end; that's what defines you and gives you the power to transfer wealth to the next generation. Activate your real estate mind and find out how to transform your passion into generational wealth. Demonstrate your confidence, believing that what is inside of you can become reality.

Chapter 12
God's Plan

We are all created different, from race, sex, religion, height, and size. We all view life differently, based on how we see the world through our experiences. One thing we all share in common is that we all have a gift that can impact the world. We all are made with a gift inside of us that speaks to us in our dreams, when we are awake, or when we are sitting at the desk at that job that frustrates us but is paying the bills and providing food and shelter.

After 20 years of the revolving circle, I understood, there is no easy way to develop your dreams and aspirations. You must take the necessary steps to develop the gift inside you. Building was my passion, which helped me develop these step-by-step strategies that I speak of in this book, from learning your market to having an intimate relationship, to leveraging your gift. These chapters are key components that have been the soil that has helped me build my business.

The Real Estate Mind

From the first house I renovated, in which I used to cry the bucket of tears, to the home I purchased debt-free, I never allowed my passion to die. Real estate is what makes me come alive. When I'm in a home that has damaged walls, damaged floors, no furnace and boarded up windows, I'm like a kid in my own world; I see something different. I see granite countertops, marble floors, painted walls and a new furnace with central air. Can you see what's inside of you, no matter how you begin?

Life has taught me; if you tap into your infinite intelligence and follow what's in your heart, get the education you need, and work hard with your mind and your hands, you can do whatever your mind can think of. Even if you have some losses in the beginning, understand that getting to where you want to go is a process of elimination.

Activate your real estate mind, tap into your infinite intelligence, find your passion, believe in your passion, and demonstrate your passion. Real estate may not be your passion, but a tool to develop your passion. Whatever your goal is, if you follow the simple steps in this book, you will see the fruits of your labor. I challenge you to stop dreaming and take the necessary actions to act out what's inside of you. If real estate is your passion, then I want you to start setting logical goals, to make a commitment, to activate your real estate mind. If it's a tool to develop your passion, I want you to replace the word real estate and put in there what makes you come alive and begin the process of activation of what GOD put inside of you.

1. Learn your market - every move you make look to capitalize by gaining knowledge and capital.

2. Strategy - build a strong foundation to withstand any adversity.

3. Build a team - surround yourself around individuals that understand there's no "I" in team and who are great at things that you are not.

4. Intimate relationship with your finances - learn the value of money and spend it on things that give you a return and not on things that decrease in value.

5. Emotionless game plan - don't sign a check or make an Investment based on emotions, if you want your business to grow, stand on this one thought; if you're not doing charity don't waste your time with thoughts that will not increase you mentally or financially.

6. Revolving Circle - don't become complacent, stay humble and let every event in your life build you, and understand losing is part of the process.

7. Leverage - build a team that shares common goals and that have found there passion in areas that you are not great in, which are essential to your growth.

8. Giving - follow the steps of learning how to be fruitful, multiply, replenish and subdue.

9. Rich vs. Wealth - transform your thinking to learn how to build wealth versus investing in material things to only seeking approval from the world that will die with leaving bills instead of assets for there family.

10. Confidence - what ever makes you come alive believe in that and learn how to develop it into a career or business by obtaining direct education. If a person that breathes the same air as you created a way to be successful and God said we are all heirs, than you have the power to create your own way.

11. God's Plan - once you find your passion, learn how to be a vessel for God that emulates his love and gives you joy.

www.ingramcontent.com/pod-product-compliance
Lightning Source LLC
Chambersburg PA
CBHW031536210526
45464CB00003B/1042